Absolute
Beginners'
Concertina

A new guide to playing the

Twenty Key Anglo Concertina

Devised and edited by Mick Bramich

Posset Press

©2000

Absolute Beginners' Concertina

a new guide to playing the twenty key Anglo concertina.

Published in England, 2000 by

Posset Press

6 Denys Road, Totnes, Devon, TQ9 5TJ, England.
Telephone/facsimile: +44 (0) 1803 863558
e-mail: mbramich@hotmail.com
web site: http://www.btinternet.com/~radical/mbramich/home.html

ISBN 0 9537837 0 7

Compiled and edited by Mick Bramich.
©Tablature designed and created by Mick Bramich.
Cover design by Mick Bramich
Printed in England by In Focus,Totnes,Devon,UK. 01803 867494

Text in 10/12 pt. Garamond and laid out in QuarkXPress

CONTENTS

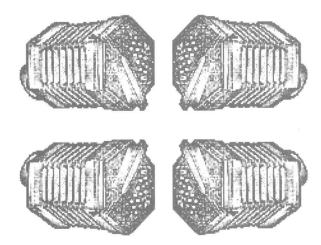

What is an Anglo Concertina?

This often asked question deserves some serious answers. There are many people who own musical instruments without necessarily knowing what they possess. Concertina owners are no exception to the rule and in order to make any progress with an instrument, it is essential to have some knowledge of its function and capabilities. The commonest misunderstandings surround the type of system that the concertina comes equipped with. The simple 20 button Anglo is probably the easiest to describe and identify as all the other available systems display many more buttons on each end of the instrument.

TOPS are the wooden or metal plates in which the buttons are located. **BUTTONS** are usually made from bone and are off-white in colour, sometimes with brown streaks where the buttons protrude from the tops.

STRAPS are a particular shape on the Anglo concertina but they can be confused with the hand straps of the **DUET** concertina. Anglos always have an extra button on one end which is used to control the flow of air through the **BELLOWS**. On a 20 button Anglo, the bellows will normally have five **FOLDS** , occasionally more when the bellows have been replaced. Most bellows are decorated with printed papers the commonest being a design of stars on a white background. Due to the old age of many of the instruments the clarity of the paper design cannot be guaranteed.

The Anglo is **HEXAGONAL** or six sided. Many English concertinas have eight or twelve sides as do the larger duets. The material used in the construction of the least expensive Anglos is mahogany, the insides being of pine. Some rare, better quality instruments have either rosewood or ebony construction and, even more scarce, metal tops with fine fretwork. The latter variety are very limited in number and are extremely valuable in comparison to the common mahogany versions.

The ultimate way to check if the concertina that you own, or plan to purchase, is an Anglo, is to allow some air into the bellows and push a button. When you pull that same button you should hear a different note. Make sure that you press a button from one of the two main rows on each end and not the **AIR BUTTON**. This button will only exhibit the sound of air being drawn into or pushed out of the bellows.

Each button sounds a different note on either of the scales available on the instrument. Pushing the air out of the bellows will sound one note and pulling the air in will sound another.

Therefore ■ = a pushed note and ❑ = a pulled note. The spare button on the right hand side is an air button.

❀❀❀❀❀❀❀❀❀❀❀❀

Figure 1. The layout of a twenty keyed Anglo concertina. This can vary from make to make.

button	5	4	3	2	1		1	2	3	4	5
C row	■❑	■❑	■❑	■❑	■❑		■❑	■❑	■❑	■❑	■❑
	CG	GB	CD	EF	GA		CB	ED	GF	CA	EB
button	5	4	3	2	1		1	2	3	4	5
G row	■❑	■❑	■❑	■❑	■❑		■❑	■❑	■❑	■❑	■❑
	BA	DF#	GA	BC	DE		GF#	BA	DC	GE	F#F

.........Left hand side....... ....Right hand side..........

■❑ Air control

If you have a concertina which sounds like it should be an Anglo but has more than 20 buttons, then it could still be an Anglo but with a different configuration on each end. Anglos range from 20 to about 50 buttons, the most usual being 20, 26 and 30. This tutor will suit any Anglo concertina as long as you do not venture onto the **ACCIDENTAL ROWS**. These are the rows of extra buttons which occur, usually, on the outside edge of the instrument, the row furthest from your fingers. My other published tutor, **THE IRISH CONCERTINA** , covers the method for extending your playing style on the thirty button instrument.

CONCERTINA MAKERS

Any introduction to the Anglo must include some advice and tips on the types of instrument that you may come into contact with. Each make has its advantages and drawbacks and some knowledge of these facets will help you to purchase the right instrument for you, or assess whether the one that you have just dusted off after twenty years in the attic, is in fact any good for the purpose of learning the absolute basics.

I will start with the most numerous and introduce the London made concertinas of **LOUIS LACHENAL**. These are the Model T 's of the Anglo market. They were made in their hundreds of thousands over a period spanning the last half of the nineteenth century and they continued in production until the nineteen twenties. I have a price list from the maker dating from the early twentieth century and they vary from a few shillings for the basic 20 button in mahogany finish to £16. 10s. 0d. for the top of the range models. The bottom of the market Lachenal is not a very user friendly package. They are not efficient in the use of air; the action of the reeds is slow making rapid passage playing extremely difficult; they are short on bellows which adds more problems to the task of controlling air. On the positive side they are still relatively inexpensive despite being many times dearer now than when they started life.

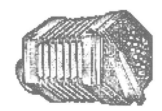

To place some sort of perspective on the price increase of these instruments, I will illustrate by giving the new cost in 1900 of the basic model at £2. 16s. 0d. (which is equivalent to £2.80) compared with the 1999 price of about £180 to £280 dependent upon condition. Rosewood and metal topped versions can fetch up to £600.00.

I will deal with the other makers very briefly. Of the old names in the business, only **Jones** made any impression on the stranglehold of **Lachehal** in the market place. They tend to be a little unwieldy with large buttons and poor air efficiency. They are priced similarly to Lachenal products. **Wheatstone** made some cracking instruments but do not expect to find a twenty keyed version. Likewise, the names of **Charles Jeffries** and **Jeffries Brothers** are associated with top quality concertinas and a few twenties may still be encountered although the smallest you are more likely to see is of twenty six buttons. They are expensive at around £750.00 or more. Furthermore, the bellows will be far superior on these more expensive instruments.

Of the modern versions, few are to be recommended unless you intend to start out with little hope of achieving the true concertina sound. The product of the Italian or German accordion makers, these instruments are built with piano accordion type construction, the reeds being set in parallel pans as opposed to the radial layout of a true concertina. Consequently, the sound suffers and repairs are time consuming. Makers of real concertinas do not bother with the twenty key as they see the only real option in terms of production efficiency and sales with the thirty plus configurations. In price, the mock concertina is cheap at less than a hundred pounds; the modern craftsman made versions begin at about £800.00.

BUYING A CONCERTINA

When contemplating the purchase of a concertina, several factors must be taken into account. If cost is the major consideration then the simplest advice is to spend the most that you can afford. Buying a better instrument at the outset will almost guarantee success in overcoming the early stages of the learning process. As already mentioned, the cheap and cheerful concertinas have some drawbacks.

There are two main avenues for the potential buyer.   1. Mail order and 2. Stalls at festivals where traditional music predominates.

The first method is great if you know exactly what you want and are dealing with a responsible retailer. The second is without doubt the method to go for. What better chance to have a rake of instruments in front of you and the opportunity to try them at your leisure and discuss the various merits of each item that takes your fancy. It is also cheaper in the long term. There is no costly postage and insurance, no finding out that you may have picked a dodo and plenty of time to consider the options fully before parting with your hard earned cash.

The keys available on the basic 20 key instrument are generally C major, G major, A minor, E minor, a limited access to D minor and B minor and a likewise curtailed F major. This does not detract from the instruments usefulness however and many a good tune or song accompaniment can be coaxed from this simple but rewarding little box of steel, wood and leather.

The next section deals with the playing of the basic keys and does not presume that the player has any foreknowledge of the methods to be employed.

The concertina in comfortable surroundings – the pub where music sessions abound!

It really is aimed at the absolute beginner and the range of tunes used in each instructional phase are very easy indeed and in some cases, very well known so that the player has an idea of how the melody should sound already in their head.

Good luck with your learning and ultimately, your playing. Your technique will improve with practice but if you begin to feel any form of discomfort in your hands then take a break. New usage of dormant muscles can aggravate the player at the outset.

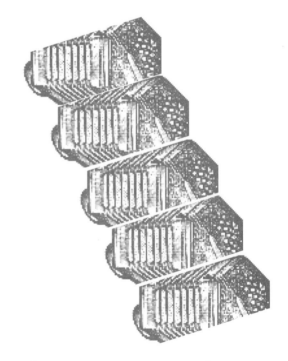

Anglo concertinas are good for jugglers!

THE KEY OF C MAJOR

The commonest keys found on the twenty button Anglo are C major and G major. The notes of these diatonic scales are found on the two rows.

Figure 2.   The scale of C major.

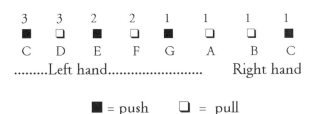

3	3	2	2	1	1	1	1
■	❑	■	❑	■	❑	❑	■
C	D	E	F	G	A	B	C

.........Left hand.........................   Right hand

■ = push   ❑ = pull

Try this simple run up the scale of C major. This is the row of buttons furthest away from the handstraps.

You will see that each button has two available notes, one in each direction of the bellows. Button 3 on the left hand side gives a C when pushed and a D when pulled. Likewise, number 1 on the right hand side gives B when pulled and C when pushed. The C on the right is one octave above the starting point on the third button on the left. Practice the action of pushing and pulling the scale of C major in just one octave. Remember to continue with the pulling action when changing from the left hand side to the right hand side of the instrument.

Do not attempt to play any tunes at this early stage of the proceedings. By jumping ahead you may miss some important factors employed in the method being taught. Keep practicing this exercise until you feel comfortable with the key of C major.

Now try working down the scale from the high C to the lower octave C in the left hand. The direction of the bellows action is identical. Once more, keep practicing; do not be tempted to jump ahead yet.

THE KEY OF G MAJOR

G major is the next key to tackle if only to get you used to working on a different row with the same movements of the fingers and the bellows.

Figure 3.

3	3	2	2	1	1	1	1
■	❑	■	❑	■	❑	❑	■
G	A	B	C	D	E	F #	G

---------Left----------------------   -Right-

■ = push   ❑ =   pull

Just as in the key of C major, try to play the scale of G starting with the third button on the left hand side on the row nearest to your fingers. Notice that the bellows are to be pulled when you change from the left hand to the right hand. When you feel confident with this exercise, try going down the scale from the high G to the G on the left hand side one octave below.

You may have seen that a sharpened note occurs in the key of G. The note is F# and it is the first button pulled on the right hand side. Throughout the tutor, the simple device of ■ = push and ❑ = pull will be used for all exercises and practice tunes. So now let us take a look at a couple of melodies which can be played within the scope of what you have learned so far.

A well known tune to practice is 'When the Saints go marching in' as it is contained within one octave. Here it is in tablature form with the simple push and pull devices to guide you. This is the C row.

3   2   2   1 /   3   2   2   1 /
■   ■   ☐   ■   ■   ■   ☐   ■

C   E   F   G   rest   C   E   F   G   rest

3   2   2   1 /   2   3   2   3 /
■   ■   ☐   ■   ■   ■   ■   ☐

C   E   F   G   E   C   E   D   rest

2   2   2   3   2   1   1   2 ....
■   ■   ☐   ■   ■   ■   ■   ☐

E   E   F   C   long   E   G   G   F   long

2   2   1   2   3   3   3 ....
■   ☐   ■   ■   ■   ☐   ■

E   F   G   E   C   D   C   long.

A rest in just what it describes; it is a brief rest where no sound is made. Long means that you hold the note for a longer period of time, in this tune about three times longer than the short notes.

All the movement is on the left hand side of the instrument and the regular changes in the direction of the bellows should not give you any problems with too much or too little air to play the melody with. Practice the piece until it is fluent and a friend (a good friend!) can recognise it.

Now you can play the same tune on the G row of the concertina. The finger positions are the same but on the row nearest to the handstraps. The notes played will obviously be different and the tune will be a fifth higher in pitch, that is, five whole notes or tones above the original pitch.

Simplicity itself! Practice the tune in the key of G major and keep going back to C major to remind yourself of the first way of playing it. The 'interval' between the two keys is the musical way of stating the difference between them. In this case the interval is a fifth. To find this figure, take C as one and count up to G; five should be the answer or in musical terms again, a fifth.

C	D	E	F	G
1	2	3	4	5

The next exercise will bring the right hand into the method of playing. Once again, a simple, well known tune will be used as an example.

THE COCK OF THE NORTH
in the key of C major

2   2   2   3   3   2   2   1   1   1
■   ■   ■   ☐   ■   ■   ☐   ■   ☐ .... ■

E   E   E   D   C   E   F   G   A   long   G

2   2   2   3   3   3
■   ■   ■   ☐   ■   ☐ ....

E   E   E   D   C   D   long

2   2   2   3   3   2   2   1   1   1
■   ■   ■   ☐   ■   ■   ☐   ■   ☐ .....   ■

E   E   E   D   C   E   F   G   A   long   G

2   2   3   3   3   3 ....
■   ■   ☐   ■   ☐   ■

E   E   D   C   D   C   long.

1R   1L   1L   1L   1R   1L   1L   1L
■   ■   ☐   ■   ■   ■   ☐   ■

C   G   A   G   C   G   A   G

2   2   2   3   3   3
■   ■   ■   ☐   ■   ☐ ....

E   E   E   D   C   D   long.

1R   1L   1L   1L   1R   1L   1L   1L
■   ■   ☐   ■   ■   ■   ☐   ■

C   G   A   G   C   G   A   G

2   2   3   2   3   3
■   ■   ☐   ■   ☐   ■ ....

E   E   D   E   D   C   long.

In this tune you will see the symbols R and L which shows you when to move to the right hand side of the concertina and when to stay on the left. If no symbol is present, then assume that the left hand is intended. As before, long means about three times the length of the regular notes in the melody.

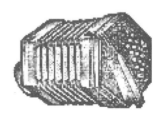

EXTENDING THE SCALES

Most tunes are greater than one octave in range, In other words, they stretch beyond the limits that the previous exercises show. The next step is to learn to play with more right hand and to extend the notes of the scale to increase the numbers of tunes that you can play. The diagrams show the extended scales of both C major and G major in the right hand.

Figure 4. Extended scales of C and G.

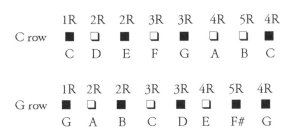

C row	1R	2R	2R	3R	3R	4R	5R	4R
	■	❑	■	❑	■	❑	❑	■
	C	D	E	F	G	A	B	C

G row	1R	2R	2R	3R	3R	4R	5R	4R
	■	❑	■	❑	■	❑	■	■
	G	A	B	C	D	E	F#	G

Can you spot the difference between the way of playing the scale of C and the scale of G? On either row you have to travel to the fifth button and then come back to the fourth to complete the octave (eight notes). On the G row, the fourth and fifth buttons are played in different directions to the buttons on the C row. It is tricky to remember these differences all the time so practice with care in both scales.

Similarly, as shown in figure 5, the scale goes below the middle C or G on each row in the left hand but not in as complete a form as in the right hand.

Figure 5.

C row	5	5	4	4	3
	■	❑	■	❑	■
	C	G	G	D	C

G row	5	5	4	4	3
	■	❑	■	❑	■
	D	A	G	F#	B

The scales have large gaps in them but the progressions should still be practiced and learned. These lower notes can be used successfully in the construction of **CHORDS**.

These are groups of notes, often three in a group, which, when played together, produce a harmonic sound which is related to the scales available on the instrument. Most chord playing on the Anglo can be achieved on the left hand side. Here are a few chords showing the finger positions and which fingers to play them with.

X marks the buttons which are not played.

	5	4	3	2	1	
C row	X	X	■	■	■	= C major , pushed chord.
Fingers			3	2	1	

	5	4	3	2	1	
C row	X	■	X	X	X	
		1				
G row	■	■	X	X	X	= G major , pushed chord.
	3	2				

	5	4	3	2	1	
C row	X	X	X	❑	X	
				1		
G row	X	X	❑	❑	X	= F major , pulled chord.
			3	2		

	5	4	3	2	1	
G row	X	X	■	■	■	= G major , pushed chord.
			3	2	1	

These four chords are useful when playing in the key of C major as they are all **RELATED** to each other within the scale. More chords which are available on the twenty buttoned instrument are shown on page 21.

Here is one more tune to practice in the major scales. Try to play it without knowing the title and see if you recognise it after a couple of times through it. The answer is at the foot of page 11 if you cannot wait or even worse, you do not know the tune! *

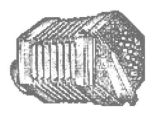

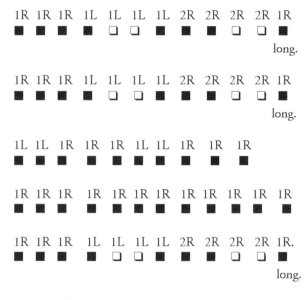

1R 1R 1R 1L 1L 1L 1L 2R 2R 2R 2R 1R
■   ■   ■   ■   □   □   ■   ■   ■   □   □   ■
                                              long.

1R 1R 1R 1L 1L 1L 1L 2R 2R 2R 2R 1R
■   ■   ■   ■   □   ■   ■   ■   ■   □   □   ■
                                              long.

1L 1L 1R 1R 1R 1L 1L 1R 1R 1R
■   ■   ■   ■   ■   □   ■   ■   ■   ■

1R 1R 1R 1R 1R 1R 1R 1R 1R 1R 1R 1R
■   ■   ■   ■   ■   ■   ■   ■   ■   ■   ■   ■

1R 1R 1R 1L 1L 1L 1L 2R 2R 2R 2R 1R.
■   ■   ■   ■   □   □   ■   ■   ■   □   □   ■
                                              long.

Try the same tune on the G row. It will sound a little more harsh because the notes are one fifth higher in pitch. This is rather like asking a baritone singer to change to a high tenor voice. It may be an old chestnut but it is a good exercise in the control of air into and out of the bellows.

SOME TIPS ON MAINTENANCE

As mentioned earlier, many of the twenty keyed instruments were considered to be not much better than toys in their heyday and the quality of construction suffered accordingly. Air is required to drive the reed under the button that has been pressed. If the bellows are at full stretch and you need to pull a note, then you must allow some air into the bellows. You should try and pre-plan these inductions of air so that you do not place the bellows under stress; they could be of a considerable age and liable to breakdown if worked too hard.

Allowing air to escape from the bellows on a pushed note is a good way of preventing the stretching process. Likewise, admitting air when pulling notes is useful if the next passage contains lots of pushed notes. Only practice with the air button and getting used to your own instrument will determine which methods you adopt for the control of air.

To make a note sound quieter, try half opening the air button while pushing or pulling

a note. Repeat the note without air button and you should notice an audible difference in the volume.

At the outset, it would be wise to ensure that the instrument is as air efficient as age and condition allows. New pads, which prevent the note sounding until the button above it is pressed, are cheap and easy to fit (see list of suppliers). Springs must all be of a similar tension so that the pads are not forced to open by the pressure of air in the bellows.

Sticking buttons can be readily removed and cleaned of any foreign matter that may be causing them to jam in their holes. Each reed also has a valve, a simple flap of leather or plastic material, which are sometimes found to be in the open position when the concertina is inspected. This is usually the result of the instrument being stored in a vertical position over many years. An Anglo, or any other concertina, should be stored horizontally with the flats of the hexagonal sides downwards.

Bellows are often 'holed', that is, they have tiny perforations or even gaping gashes in them. Large holes are easier to remedy than pin pricks simply by using thin strips of leather and a suitable adhesive such as PVA or UHU. Always try to patch bellows on the inside to prevent unsightly and cumbersome bulges on the exterior of the concertina.

Finally, always place your Anglo in a box so as to keep it clean and store it in a place which is not close to radiators or other sources of heat as a reasonable humidity level is important in preventing splitting or distortion.

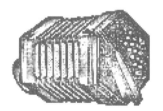

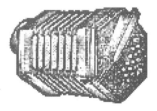

MINOR KEYS

The twenty button Anglo can also produce scales for two minor keys, A minor and E minor. They are not the scales which are known to trained musicians as **HARMONIC** and **MELODIC** scales. The scales as they occur on the concertina are closer to the ones found in **MODES**. Without getting too technical, modes determine the intervals, or gaps, between the notes of the scale. There are two modes in each minor scale on the twenty buttoned variety and they are known by their Greek names of **DORIAN** and **AEOLIAN**.

Figure 6. A minor Aeolian

	1L	1R	1R	2R	2R	3R	3R	4R
C row	❑	❑	■	❑	■	❑	■	❑
	A	B	C	D	E	F	G	A

In its simplest form, most of the notes are played on the right hand side. The regular change in direction of the bellows will not create too many problems with air control. Practice the scale in both directions, that is rising and falling scale, until it begins to feel comfortable.

Figure 7. A minor Dorian

	1L	1R	1R	2R	2R
C row	❑	❑	■	❑	■
	A	B	C	D	E

	1R	1R	2R
G row	❑	■	❑
	F#	G	A

You will see from this diagram of the scale that you must cross to the G row to find all the notes of the octave. This is a trick which should be learned from the very start as it will have implications if you choose at some point to progress to a thirty buttoned instrument. The scale sounds different because of the inclusion of the F note which is sharpened. This changes the intervals within the scale. These types of scales are common in **TRADITIONAL MUSIC** and it is not unusual to see the Anglo is situations where this kind of music persists, for example, Morris dancing, ceilidhs and pub sessions at folk festivals.

In order to practice the scale of A minor, it will be necessary to introduce some simple, traditional tunes into this section. They may or may not be familiar but you should be able to hear them clearly if you follow the tablature accurately. The one thing that I have not introduced yet is the length of a note or its **VALUE**. This is a bit of mathematics which could help you if you have no prior knowledge of musical theory.

Note	Shape	Value
Semi-breve	o	1
Minim	♩	1/2
Crotchet	♩	1/4
Quaver	♪	1/8

Shown as fractions of a semi-breve.

These examples will be enough to help you through the easy tunes in this book. Most traditional melodies only contain crotchets and quavers which simplifies the situation. A crotchet can be any length that you choose but a quaver should always be half the length of the crotchet.

The length of the notes will now be included on the tablature. This does mean that you have to absorb several pieces of information at once in order to play the tune. Just take your time. There is no need to rush through the pieces.

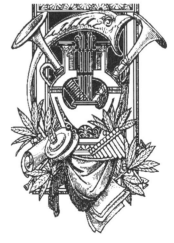

*Old McDonald had a Farm.

NONESUCH (4/4)

This tune has a time signature of 4/4 which means that it has four beats of the same value in each of the 16 bars of music. Tap out a rhythm of 1, 2, 3, 4; 1, 2, 3, 4; 1, 2, 3, 4; etc.. until you feel confident enough to try the tablature.

Value of note:

♩ ♩ ♩ ♩ ♩ ♩ ♪ ♪ ♩

■ ■ ■ □ ■ ■ □ ■ □

C row 2R 2R 1R 2R 2R 1R 1R 1R 1L

♩ ♩ ♩ ♩ ♩ ♩ ♩

■ ■ ■ □ ■ ■ □

C row 2R 2R 1R 2R 2R 1R 1L

♩ ♩ ♩ ♩ ♩ ♩ ♪ ♪ ♩

■ ■ ■ □ ■ ■ □ ■ □

C row 2R 2R 1R 2R 2R 1R 1R 1R 1L

♩ ♩ ♩ ♩ ♩ ♩ ♩

■ ■ ■ □ ■ ■ □

C row 2R 2R 1R 2R 2R 1R 1L

♩ ♩ ♩ ♩ ♩ ♩ ♪ ♪ ♩

□ □ ■ □ □ ■ □ ■ □

C row 1R 1R 1L 1L 1R 1R 1R 1R 1L

♩ ♩ ♩ ♩ ♩ ♩ ♩

□ □ ■ □ □ ■ □

C row 1R 1R 1L 1L 1R 1R 1L

♩ ♩ ♩ ♩ ♩ ♩ ♪ ♪ ♩

□ □ ■ □ □ □ ■ □ □

C row 1R 1R 1L 1L 1R 1R 1R 1R 1L

♩ ♩ ♩ ♩ ♩ ♩ ♩

□ □ ■ □ □ ■ □

C row 1R 1R 1L 1L 1R 1R 1L

Your first tune in A minor does not contain the note of F and so the mode is not determined. It is a dance tune from Playford's 'Dancing Master' of 1651. The E minor scale, Aeolian mode, uses the F# note which is a pull on the fourth button of the G row in the left hand. The instrument does not contain any C sharp notes.

Figure 8. E minor Aeolian

2L 4L 1L 1L 1R 1R 2R 2R

■ □ ■ □ □ ■ □ ■

E F# G A B C D E

G row

BUSHES AND BRIARS (3/4)

♩ ♪ ♪ ♪♪ ♪ ♩ ♩♪.

■ □ ■ □ □ ■ □

G row 2L 1L 1L 1L 1R 1L 1L

♪ ♪ ♪ ♩ ♪ ♪ ♩♩

□ ■ □ ■ □ ■ □

G row 1R 1R 2R 2R 2R 1R 1R

♪ ♪ ♩♩ ♪ ♪ ♪ ♩♩ ♩ ♩♩ ♪ ♪ ♩♩

■ □ ■ □□ ■ □□ □ ■ ■

1R 2R 2R 2R 1R 1R 1R 1L 1R 1L 2L

G row

♪ ♪ ♪ ♩♩♪ ♩♩ ♪ ♪ ♩♩

□ □ ■ ■ □ ■ □

G row 3L 3L 2L 1R 1R 1R 1R 1L

This well known song tune is a good exercise in the key of E minor but it can also be played on the C row with the same fingering technique. The next tune reverts to G major but it is longer and the note values are a little harder to follow. It needs plenty of practice to get it right.

THE WILD ROVER

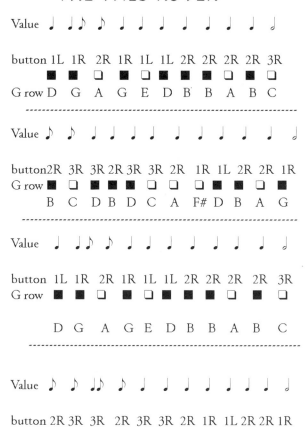

```
Value  ♩  ♩♪  ♪   ♩  ♩  ♩  ♩  ♩  ♩  ♩  ♩  𝅗𝅥

button 1L 1R 2R 1R 1L 1L 2R 2R 2R 2R 3R
       ■  ■  ❑  ■  ❑  ■  ■  ■  ❑  ■  ❑
G row D  G  A  G  E  D  B  B  A  B  C
------------------------------------------------

Value  ♪  ♪  ♩  ♩  ♩  ♩  ♩  ♩  ♩  ♩  ♩  𝅗𝅥

button 2R 3R 3R 2R 3R 3R 2R 1R 1L 2R 2R 1R
G row ■  ❑  ■  ■  ❑  ❑  ❑  ■  ■  ❑  ■
      B  C  D  B  D  C  A  F# D  B  A  G
------------------------------------------------

Value  ♩  ♩♪  ♪   ♩  ♩  ♩  ♩  ♩  ♩  ♩  ♩  𝅗𝅥

button 1L 1R 2R 1R 1L 1L 2R 2R 2R 2R 3R
G row ■  ■  ❑  ■  ❑  ■  ■  ■  ❑  ■  ❑

      D  G  A  G  E  D  B  B  A  B  C
------------------------------------------------

Value  ♪  ♪  ♩♪  ♪   ♩  ♩  ♩  ♩  ♩  ♩  ♩  𝅗𝅥

button 2R 3R 3R 2R 3R 3R 2R 1R 1L 2R 2R 1R

G row ■  ❑  ■  ■  ■  ❑  ❑  ❑  ■  ■  ❑  ■
      B  C  D  B  D  C  A  F# D  B  A  G
```

This will need considerably more practice than the earlier tunes before it begins to sound 'right'. It can be played with exactly the same fingering on the C row. By learning just to read the push and pull devices, you will achieve greater speed and fluency with the tune and be able to transfer most tunes between the rows.

Another minor scale that can be attempted is that of D minor. The twenty button instrument can only play the scale in the Dorian mode because there is not a Bb note available. Some traditional dance music occurs in this key but it is infrequently found in the better known collections.

Figure 9. The scale of D minor Dorian.

```
       3L 2L 2L 1L 1L 1R 1R 2R
C row  ❑  ■  ❑  ■  ❑  ❑  ■  ❑
       D  E  F  G  A  B  C  D
```

It can be difficult to identify tunes in this key as there are no sharps or flats to be seen on the stave. This could place the melody in C major or A minor but one way of telling which is which is to read the first few notes from the stave. If the tune starts with a D note then it is likely to be in D minor. If it starts on D and a sharp is shown on the stave, then it is probably in G major.

A couple of chords are available in this scale, those of F major and D minor, both on the left hand side.

```
button    5  4  3  2  1
C row     X  X  ❑  ❑  ❑   =  D minor, a pulled
fingers         3  2  1              chord.

          5  4  3  2  1
C row     X  X  X  ❑  X
                   1      =  F major, a pulled
                                     chord.
G row     X  X  ❑  ❑  X
                3     2
```

As mentioned before, chords are useful in the control of air, allowing you to expel or import large amounts before running out of bellows in either direction. By studying the layout of the buttons on the right hand side of your Anglo you will be able to find another octave in D minor. In order to achieve it you must cross onto the right hand G row to locate the note of D to conclude the scale. It is a pushed note on the third button on the G row. If you have a good memory for the tunes you have already practiced, try to convert them into D minor. Remember though, only Dorian mode tunes can be played in this key.

ENTABULATING MELODIES

Part of the joy involved in learning to play a different instrument evolves from the tasks which you can set for yourself so as to further improve your knowledge and understanding of musical processes. The method which displays the tunes and scales in this book is known as **TABLATURE**. It has a long history being of far greater antiquity than the five line stave which we all recognise.

Tablature, or 'tab' for short, was employed to suit different instruments and it is still used today in the teaching of guitar and in France, for melodeon tuition.

If you are not a reader of staff notation, then you can quite simply **ENTABULATE** your own tunes into the system of 'tab' for the Anglo. You will need to know a few basics of staff notation but only what the notes are called and where they fall upon the stave.

Figure 10. Stave with notes from the concertina marked.

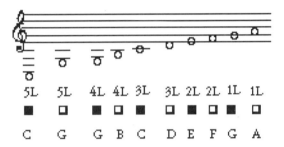

All buttons on C row, left hand.

The note values can be written in above the button numbers. By making your own chart of notes and positions on your instrument, you can start to develop your own entabulated tunes.

By employing this method, you can build up a library of melodies in a very short time without the need to go deeper into music theory. This could be criticised as taking short cuts but in my experience, most amateur performers want rapid results. They cannot achieve those results if they have to bury themselves in mounds of paperwork from dusty library shelves simply to satisfy musical theorists

that they are taking the right path to their chosen hobby. The majority of people who play traditional music have managed very well without the heavy burden of theory and possibly enjoy their music making much more as a result. This does not make music theory redundant; it puts in into the background for further investigation when you feel that you are ready for it.

YOUR ANGLO CONCERTINA

It would be a useful exercise for you to make a chart of the buttons on your instrument and the notes that they sound when pulled or pushed. Here is a blank layout which will enable you to fill in the notes as they occur on your Anglo. It is worth mentioning that many instruments have been altered by their original owners or later restorers and they may not display the conventional layout. This can easily be remedied by the mechanically minded or very inexpensively by a recognised repairer or maker of concertinas.

The reeds fit snugly into dovetailed slots in the reed pan and are removed with slight pressure from the fingers. They usually have the note letter stamped onto the brass shoe which holds the vibrating reed. These can be misleading because they may have been altered by a semi-tone or more during their lifetime by successive re-tunings of the instrument. It is useful to compare the pitch of the reed with another known true pitch sound such as that from a piano, electronic keyboard or tuning fork. This is done by blowing through the reed with the mouth.

Fill in this chart to help you with your entabulation of tunes.

button	5	4	3	2	1		1	2	3	4	5
C row	■□	■□	■□	■□	■□		■□	■□	■□	■□	■□
Notes	-----	-----	-----	-----	-----		------	------	-------	------	------
button	5	4	3	2	1		1	2	3	4	5
G row	■□	■□	■□	■□	■□		■□	■□	■□	■□	■□
Notes	------	-------	------	------	-----		------	------	------	------	------

LEFT HAND SIDE   * Air button RIGHT HAND SIDE

A SELECTION OF TUNES FOR THE TWENTY BUTTON ANGLO CONCERTINA

A few simple melodies which will fit either the twenty buttoned concertina or any of the larger format Anglo system instruments should be added so that you do not have to start entabulating tunes from the very outset. It is as a response to the point made earlier about people wanting rapid, if not instant, results from their chosen instrument. The majority of the tunes are traditional and can be found among the pages of many collections, some of which are listed on page 22.

The time signature of each tune is given at the beginning of every entabulation. 4/4 or C should be counted out as 1, 2, 3, 4, 1, 2, 3, 4, etc,. 6/8 should be 1, 2, 3, 4, 5, 6, and 3/4 as 1, 2, 3, 1, 2, 3, etc,. Another way to remember 6/8 time is to follow the example of bodhran players and tap out any series of three syllabled names such as 'Liverpool, Everton, Liverpool, Everton'. The choice of these two famous names from Association Football implies no bias on my part! Happy playing and even happier days working with 'tab'!

SHE MOVED THROUGH THE FAIR (3/4) ~ C row

1L	1L	1R	1R	1R	1R	2R	2R	1R	1L	2L	1L	1L	1L
■	□	□	■	□	■	□	□	■	□	□	■	■	■
G	A	B	C	B	C	D	D	C	A	F	G	G	G

2R	2R	3R	3R	2R	2R	2R	1R	1R	1R	1R	2R
□	■	□	■	□	■	□	□	■	□	■	□
D	E	F	G	D	E	D	B	C	B	C	D

2R	2R	3R	3R	2R	2R	2R	1R	1R	1R	1R	2R
□	■	□	■	□	■	□	□	■	□	■	□
D	E	F	G	D	E	D	B	C	B	C	D

1L	1L	1R	1R	1R	1R	2R	2R	1R	1L	2L	1L	1L	1L
■	□	□	■	□	■	□	□	■	□	□	■	■	■
G	A	B	C	B	C	D	D	C	A	F	G	G	G

This haunting Irish air has an equally expressive set of words some of which were probably added to the tune early in the twentieth century. The bar lines may help sight reading musicians to play the tune on another instrument.

SWEET JENNY JONES (3/4)
Played on the C row

1L	1R	1L	2L	3L	3L	2L	2L	1L	2R	1R	1L	1R
■	■	■	■	■	□	■	□	□	□	□	■	□
G	C	G	E	C	D	E	F	A	D	B	G	B

1R	1L	2L		2L	1L	1L		1L	1R	1R		1R		Repeat the first two lines
■	■	■		□	■	□		■	■	□		■		
C	G	E		F	G	A		G	C	B		C		

1R	2R	2R	1R	2R		2R	1R	1L		1R	1R	1R		1R	1L	1R	2R
■	□	■	■	■		□	□	■		■	□	■		□	■	■	□
C	D	E	C	E		D	B	G		C	A	C		B	G	C	D

2R	1R	2R		2R	1R	1L		1R	1R	1L		1L	1L	1R
■	■	■		□	□	■		■	□	□		■	□	□
E	C	E		D	B	G		C	B	A		G	A	B

1R	1L	2L		3L	3L	2L		2L	1L	2R		1R	1L	1R
■	■	■		■	□	■		□	□	□		□	■	□
C	G	E		C	D	E		F	A	D		B	G	B

1R	1L	2L		2L	1L	1L		1L	1R	1R		1R
■	■	■		□	■	□		■	■	□		■
C	G	E		F	G	A		G	C	B		C

This waltz time tune is found widely in the English tradition. This particular version is a Morris dance melody from Adderbury in Oxfordshire. There are many ancient survivals within the corpus of Morris dance music and the next tune dates back to at least the middle of the sixteenth century in a more elaborate form called 'La Mourisque'. The version from Headington Quarry, which was probably introduced from the revived Bidford side of 1886, is used as a 'Morris Off' to round off a set of dances and to process away to the next venue.

Bampton Morris, 1970

MORRIS OFF (C OR 4/4)
Played on the G row

♩ ♩ ♩ ♩ | ♫♫ ♩ | ♩ ♩ ♩ ♩ | ♫♫ ♫ :||

1L	1L	1L	1L		1L	2L		2L	3L	3L	3L	4L	4L
■	■	■	□		■	□		■	■	■	□	□	■
D	D	D	E		D	C		B	G	G	A	F#	D

♩ ♩ ♩ ♩ | ♩ ♩ ♩ ♩ | ♩ ♩ ♩ ♩ | ♩♩ ♩♩ :||

2L	3L	3L	3L		2L	3L	3L	3L		2L	3L	3L	3L	4L	4L
■	■	□			■	■	■	□		■	■	□		□	■
B	G	A			B	G	G	A		B	G	G	A	F#	D

So far, all the tunes in this section have been in the major scales of C and G. Here are a couple of minor melodies with which to practice more fully the method for the Anglo concertina.

BOUREE (C OR 4/4)
Played on the G row

3
♩ ♩ ♩ ♪ ♪ ♪| ♩ ♩ ♩ ♩♩ | ♪ ♪ ♪ ♩♩ ♩ ♩ | ♩ ♩ ♩♩ |

1R	1L	1L	1R	1R	2R	1L	1L		1L	1R	1R	1R	1L	1L	2L	2L
■	□	□	□	■	□	■	■		□	□	■	□	□	■	■	■

3
♩ ♩ ♩ ♪ ♪ ♪| ♩ ♩ ♩♩ | ♪ ♪ ♪ ♩♩ ♩ | ♩ ♩ ♩♩ ||

1R	1L	1L	1R	1R	2R	1L	1L		1L	1R	1R	1R	1L		1L	2L	2L
■	□	□	□	■	□	■	■		□	□	■	□	□		■	■	■

♩ ♫♫ | ♩ ♫♫ | ♩ ♩ ♪ ♪ ♪ | ♩ ♪ ♪ | ♩ ♩ ♩ ♩ ♩|

2R	1R	2R	1R		2R	1R	2R	2R		1R	2R		2R	2R	1R	1R
■	■	■	■		■	■	□	■		■	□		■	□	□	□

♪ ♪ ♩ ♪ ♪ ♩ ♩| ♩ ♩ ♪ ♪ ♪ ♪ ♪ ♪| ♩ ♪ ♪ ♪ ♪ ♪ ♩ | ♫♫♫

1R	1R	2R	1R	1R	2R	1R	1L		1L	1R	1R	2R	2R	2R	1R	1R		1L	1R	1L
□	■	□	□	■	□	■	□		□	□	■	□	■	□	■	□		□	□	□

This ancient melody probably started life in France during the sixteenth century. It was arranged by various composers of the period for full Renaissance band and about a hundred years later, it found its way into Playford's 'Dancing Master' under the title of 'Parson's Farewell'. You will see that the line which normally gives you the name of each note has been left out. If you find this a problem then you can simply pencil the letters in. It is an attempt to reduce the amount of information that you have to read at any one time.

CUCKOOS NEST (C OR 4/4)
Played on the C row.

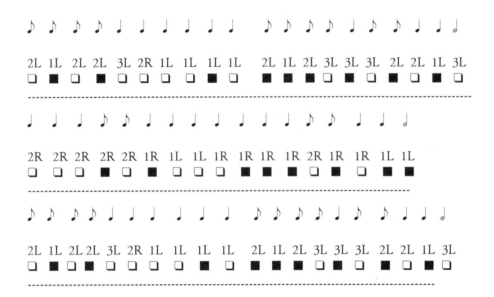

This tune is in D minor even though it is played on the C row. It has relatives in Ireland, Scotland and America and is sometimes a song tune. This variant is used by Morris dancers and it comes from Sherborne in Gloucestershire.

OUT ON THE OCEAN (6/8)
Played on the C and G rows

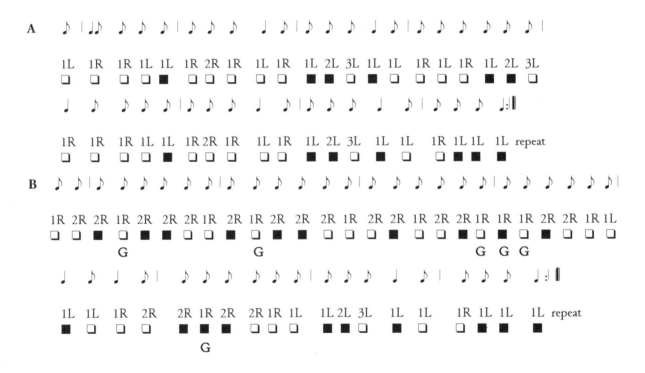

This popular jig from Ireland exploits the use of both rows to play the tune. The F# note and the G above it are played on the first button of the right hand G row. These notes are indicated by the letter **G** beneath the button symbols. The tune is of two parts, A and B, each being repeated.

IN DVLCI JVBILO ~ C ROW

3L	3L	3L	2L	2L	1L	1L	1L	3L	3L	2L	2L	1L	1L	1L	1L	1L	1L	2L	2L	3L	3L	3L	2L	3L	3L	3L	2L	2L
C	C	C	E	F	G	A	G	C	C	E	F	G	A	G	G	A	G	F	E	C	D	D	E	D	C	D	E	F

1L	1L	1L	2L	2L	3L	3L	3L	2L	3L	3L	3L	2L	3L	5L	4L	3L	1L	2L	2L	2L	3L	3L	3L
G	A	G	F	E	C	D	D	E	D	C	D	E	C	A	B	C	G	F	E	E	D	D	C

(G row)

GAVDE TE ~ C ROW

1L	1L	1L	1L	1R	1R	1R	1R	1L	1L	1L	1L	1L	1R	1L	1L	1L	1R	1L	1L	1L
A	A	G	A	B	C	C	B	A	G	G	G	A	B	A	G	A	B	A	G	A

1L	1L	1L	1L	1R	1R	1L	1L	2L	2L	2L	3L	3L	3L	3L	2L	3L	2L	1L	1L	1R	1L	1R	1R	1L	1L
A	A	G	A	C	B	A	A	F	E	F	D	D	D	D	F	D	F	G	A	C	A	B	C	A	A

1L	1L	1L	1L	1R	1R	1R	1R	1L	1L	1L	1L	1L	1R	1L	1L	1L	1R	1L	1L	1L
A	A	G	A	B	C	C	B	A	G	G	G	A	B	A	G	A	B	A	G	A

THE SVSSEX CAROL ~ C ROW

2R	2R	1R	1R	2R	1R	1L	1L	1L	4L	1L	1L	1L	1R	1R	1R	1L	1L
D	D	B	C	D	B	A	G	A	F#	G	G	A	B	C	B	A	G

(G row)

2R	2R	1R	1R	2R	1R	1L	1L	1L	4L	1L	1L	1L	1R	1R	1R	1L	1L
D	D	B	C	D	B	A	G	A	F#	G	G	A	B	C	B	A	G

(G row)

1L	1L	1L	1L	1R	1R	2R	1R	1R	1L	2R	2R	2R	1R	1R	1L	1L	1L	1L
A	A	G	A	B	C	D	C	B	A	D	E	D	C	B	A	G	A	G

AN ENTABULATED TUNE ~ THE HULLICAN JIG (6/8)

As in a previous example, the notes on the G row in the right hand are shown as a **G.** You will soon begin to see how easy it can be to transfer your favourite tunes from conventional notation into concertina tablature. The only limitations are with regard to the available keys on the instrument. The twenty button concertina in C and G will only accept tunes written in C, G, A minor, E minor Aeolian mode, D minor Dorian mode and F major tunes where no Bb is apparent in the melody. If your instrument has 26 or 30 buttons, then the possibilities are almost endless although even with the chromatic system provided by these larger concertinas, there are some limitations with regard to the comfortable structures of the scales.

I hope that you have found the tutor useful as a means to exploit your concertina a little more adventurously than you may have thought possible. My previously published book, *The Irish Concertina*, takes you further along the road to discovering the many complexities of the instrument.

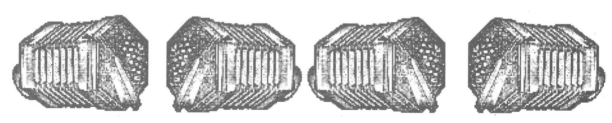

CHORDS
Pushed - left hand side

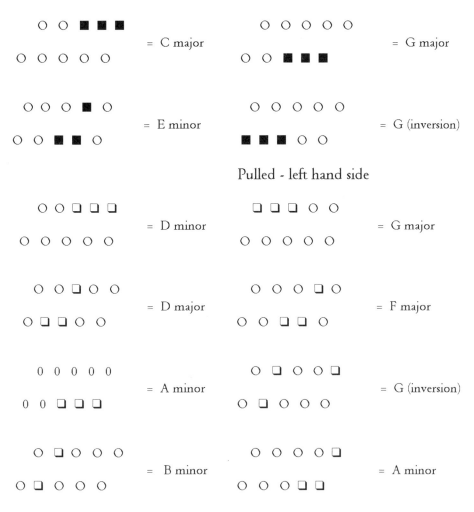

As you can see from this chart, the majority of useful chords are pulled in the left hand. By studying your instrument, you will be able to devise chord structures which incorporate the right hand as well. The patterns you discover are very good for song accompaniment.

Chords are constructed using a simple formula. The name of the chord, for example G major, gives you the starting point, the note of G. The rest of the chord is spaced from the G note as follows:

G a **B** c **D**
Root.......third........fifth

Each major chord is of this construction unless it is marked as an **INVERSION**. This means that the **TONIC** is in a different position in the chord.

For example, a first inversion of G major would be:

B c**D** e f **G**
Third....fifth.........root

A second inversion would look like this:

D e f **G** a **B**
Fifth.........root.....third

Minor chords are built in exactly the same manner for instance A minor:

A b **C** d **E**
Root.........third.......fifth

Notice that when counting the notes away from the root, that the root is included as number 1. Do not forget that chords are invaluable as a means of controlling air when the bellows become stretched or closed and you begin to run out of options!

PRINTED COLLECTIONS OF MUSIC

As you would expect, most music arrives at the printers in conventional notation, that is, five line staves with crotchets, minims, rests and all the other technicalities of printed music. The chapter in this guide on entabulating melodies does however mean that you can transfer staff notation into concertina tablature without too much difficulty. The following books of music are all traditional in character and suit the Anglo very well indeed:

The Essential Series   A collection of essential books for players of traditional music from Ireland. Dave Mallinson Publications. 1995 onwards. Titles to date: Essential; Enduring; Evergreen; Polkas. Series in progress.

The Fiddler's Tune Book   A vast collection of tunes made in the 1950's by Peter Kennedy. Another ongoing print run. Titles to date: The Fiddler's Tune Book; Reels, Rants, Flings and Fancies; Jigs and Quicksteps, Trips and Humours. Dave Mallinson Publications. 1994 onwards.

The Irish Concertina   by Mick Bramich. An advanced tutor for the thirty key Anglo concertina in the Irish style of playing. Large selection of tunes, some published for the first time. Dave Mallinson Publications. 1996.

Music for the Sets   by David Taylor. Set dance selections transcribed from recordings which accompany the series. Blue and Yellow books. Dave Mallinson Publications. 1995.

Another great source of tunes are the printed collections of Northumbrian pipe music which fit the Anglo very comfortably.

The Northumbrian Pipers' Tune Book   Various dates. Northumbrian Pipers' Society.

The Charlton Memorial Tune Book   Northumbrian Pipers' Society. 1956, reprinted 1979.

The Alnwick Pipers' Tune Book   by Ron Purvis. Alnwick Pipers' Society. 1981.

For a selection from a wide range of countries try the oddly named

One Thousand English Country Dance Tunes   by Mike Raven. Published by Mike Raven, Stafford. 1984.

INDEX OF TUNES

SUGGESTED LISTENING

The number of Anglo concertina players recorded over the last few years has greatly increased and availability is not a problem if you know where to go for your CD, cassette or even video. This list is by no means exhaustive and it includes players of many styles; some are traditional musicians and others are from the revival period of folk music. Whichever category they fall into, you can be assured that by listening to other players of the instrument, your own technique can only be improved.

Among revival English style players, there is none better than **John Kirkpatrick**. His catalogue of recordings stretches back into the early nineteen seventies and he is a crowd puller wherever he appears.

The old style of Morris musician is ably displayed on a recent EFDSS CD of **William Kimber**, noted concertina virtuoso from Headington Quarry, Oxfordshire. It was this man that set Cecil Sharp on the long road to the recovery of Morris and country dances and eventually, the traditional songs of Britain and America. EFDSS CD03 available from EFDSS at Cecil Sharp House, 2 Regent's Park Road, London, NW1 7AY.

Ireland boasts many fine players of the Anglo and amongst my favourites are the following:

Mary MacNamara - Traditional Music from East Clare CC 60CD. She plays with a delightful lilt which is at the same time both lyrical and driving.

Chris Droney - The Fertile Rock CICD 110. A great old time set dance player from the north of Clare, Chris makes the instrument sing!

Mick Bramich who devised and edited this tutor book has made recordings both as a solo artist and as a guest musician on several CD's. His own work is on **Mick Bramich** Posset PMC 103 which is a collection of traditional songs and music for the concertina and **The Irish Concertina** which is the cassette which accompanies the book of the same name from Dave Mallinson Publications. Books and cassettes are available from Posset Press, 6 Denys Road, Totnes, Devon, TQ9 5TJ. Tel/fax 01803 863558. *e mail:* mbramich@hotmail.com

Many other recordings of concertina players are available through:
Veteran Mail Order, 44 Old Street, Haughley, Stowmarket, Suffolk IP14 3NX U.K.

or fromrecorded music outlets at folk festivals and the high street shops.

Suppliers, Makers and Repairers

Concertinas are, because of their scarcity, quite expensive. Modern makers only tend to make instruments of thirty buttons or more and second hand instruments are not easily found. The following are recognised suppliers and can arrange postal shipment and trial runs:

Hobgoblin - have shops in Crawley, London, Bristol and Bradford. 07000 462462

Barleycorn Concertinas - 01782 851449

The Music Room - 35 Bradford Road, Cleckheaton, West Yorkshire, BD19 3JN.
01274 879768

Some notable makers are:

Collin Dipper - West End House, High Street, Heytesbury, Wiltshire, BA12 0EA.
01985 840516

Marcus Music - Tredegar House, Newport, Gwent. 01633 815612

A.C.Norman & Co. - Old Stables, Nursery Lane, Nutley, E. Sussex, TN 22 3NR.
01825 713551

Repairs can be carried out by the above makers and also by:

Nigel Sture - Church Gate Cottage, Malborough, Salcombe, Devon, TQ7 3RW
01548 561975

Nigel specialises in bringing back to life those exhausted concertinas that sometimes turn up in peoples lofts. He does tackle other free reed instruments but the concertina is the one that really grabs his interest.

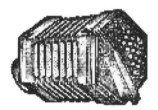

I would like to acknowledge the help of Linda Bramich who proof read the various incarnations of this book. Also two of my 'beginners', Sue Braithwaite and Dave Rushby who found the tablature easy to read and thus set them on their way to becoming Anglo players.